KINGS OF ENGLAND FOR KIDS

A History Series

Children Explore History Book Edition

SPEEDY
PUBLISHING

England is a country
that is part of the
United Kingdom.

OFFA OF MERCIA

757 - 796

was one of the leading figures of Saxon history. Offa was King of Mercia, a kingdom of Anglo-Saxon England, from 757 until his death in July 796.

EGBERT OF WESSEX

802 - 839

was King of Wessex. His
father was Ealhmund
of Kent. He conquered
the neighboring
kingdoms of Kent,
Cornwall, and Mercia.

ÆTHELWULF

839 - 856

was the son of Egbert and a sub-king of Kent. In 851 Aethelwulf defeated a Danish army at the battle of Oakley while his eldest son Althelstan fought and beat the Danes.

ÆTHELBALD OF WESSEX

856 - 860

was the second of
the five sons of King
Æthelwulf of Wessex.
He was crowned at
Kingston-upon-Thames in
southwest London, after
forcing his father to
abdicate upon his return
from pilgrimage to Rome.

ÆTHELBERHT OF WESSEX

860 - 866

was the third son of
Æthelwulf of Wessex
and his first wife,
Osburh. Like his father
and brother he was
also crowned at
Kingston upon Thames.

ÆTHELRED OF WESSEX

866 - 871

was the fourth son of King Æthelwulf of Wessex. His reign was one long struggle with the Danes who had occupied York in 866, establishing the Viking kingdom of Yorvik.

ALFRED THE GREAT

871 - 899

succeeded his brother Aethelred to the throne of Wessex in 871, and a new legal code came into force during his reign. Alfred successfully defended his kingdom against the Viking attempt at conquest.

EDWARD THE ELDER

899 - 925

became king in 899 upon the death of his father, Alfred the Great. He reconquered southeast England and the Midlands from the Danes, uniting Wessex and Mercia.

ÆTHELSTAN

925 - 940

was the son of King
Edward the Elder and
his first wife, Ecgwynn.
He defeated an invasion
by Scots, Irish, and the
men of Strathclyde at
Brunanburh in 937.

EDMUND I

940 - 946

son of Edward the Elder. He succeeded in regaining control of Mercia. He then moved on to subdue the Norsemen in Cumbria and finally extended his rule as far as southern Scotland.

EADRED

946 - 955

was a son of Edward the Elder by his third marriage, to Eadgifu. Edred enjoyed military success over the Vikings. Edred was a strongly religious man with bad health.

EADWIG

955 - 959

oldest son of King Edmund I and his Queen Ælfgifu of Shaftesbury. Eadwig's short reign was tarnished by disputes with nobles and men of the church, including Dunstan and Archbishop Oda.

EDGAR

959 - 975

King of all England from 959. He was the younger son of King Edmund I and his Queen, Ælfgifu of Shaftesbury. One of Edgar's first actions was to recall Dunstan from exile and have him made Bishop of Worcester.

EDWARD THE MARTYR

975 - 978

was the eldest son
of King Edgar the
Peaceful. Edward was
chosen as king and was
crowned by his main
clerical supporters, the
archbishops Dunstan and
Oswald of Worcester.

ÆTHELRED THE UNREADY

978 - 1016

was the son of King Edgar and Queen Ælfthryth. In 1002 he ordered the massacre of the Danish settlers, provoking an invasion by Sweyn I of Denmark.

EDMUND IRONSIDE

1016

was King of England from 23 April to 30 November 1016. Edmund's reign was marred by a war he had inherited from his father.

CNUT THE GREAT

1016 - 1035

more commonly known as Canute. Canute defeated Edmund Ironside at Assandun, Essex, in 1016, and became king of all England on Edmund's death.

HAROLD I HAREFOOT

1035 - 1040

was the younger son
of Cnut the Great. He
claimed the crown on the
death of his father, when
the rightful heir, his half-
brother Harthacnut, was
in Denmark and unable
to ascend the throne.